QU___R
UKRAINE

AN ANTHOLOGY OF LGBTQi+
UKRAINIAN VOICES DURING WARTIME

EDITED AND TRANSLATED BY
DViJKA

RENARD PRESS

RENARD PRESS LTD

124 City Road
London EC1V 2NX
United Kingdom
info@renardpress.com
020 8050 2928

www.renardpress.com

Queer Ukraine first published by Renard Press Ltd in 2023
'Ukrainian Queerness' first published on MaksymEristavi.com in 2022
'Transness in Traditional Ukrainian Culture' first published in Ukrainian as
'Transhendernist' u tradytsijnij kul'turi Ukrajiny' on update.com.ua in 2021

Text © the Authors, 2023
Translated by DViJKA
All photographs and inside illustration © Rebel Queers, 2023
Design by Will Dady

Printed in the United Kingdom by Severn

ISBN: 978-1-80447-041-1

9 8 7 6 5 4 3 2 1

All URLs accessed 1st January 2023. Renard Press has no responsibility for
the persistence or accuracy of third-party websites referenced, and does not
guarantee that any content on such websites is accurate or appropriate.

Renard Press is proud to be a climate positive publisher, removing more
carbon from the air than we emit and planting a small forest.
For more information see renardpress.com/eco.

Contents

Foreword

What do you think of when you think of queerness? Is it rainbow flags and parades, glitter and joy? Is it a corporate, sanitised version of pride, where you can only be seen if you're deemed worthy of a spotlight? Is it heart-warming coming-out stories? Is it the latest legal recognition of LGBTQI+ people's fundamental liberties?

In Ukraine, being queer is far from easy. But what is queerness if not resistance? What is queerness if not defiance? What is queerness if not the linking of arms, the echo of a hundred voices? For every voice tells a story, and every story is a thread in the grand tapestry of our existence.

Ukraine, where finding a community means salvation. Where being visibly queer is an act of rebellion. Where underground nightclubs become a bastion of solidarity. Where LGBTQI+ artists find ways to express themselves against all odds, to create beyond all constraints. Ukraine, our homeland; our beautiful, beautiful country. We've always been a part of you, and we'll always keep fighting for your freedom – no matter if our fight is twice as hard.

Ukraine, this is a love letter to you.

From the Editors

Both historically and in modern times queerness in Ukraine has meant resistance. Resistance to direct queerphobic repression and condemnation from the metropole. Resistance to its gruesome after-effects, on both a collective and individual level, on the (post)colony. Resistance against the erasure of your whole being.

If history has shown us anything, it's that during wartime, queer people are exceedingly vulnerable to persecution, scapegoating and censorship. Against the backdrop of a brutal invasion, it is much easier for conservative groups to target marginalised communities and paint them as the enemy, as a hindrance to the development of a country, completely disregarding the rich history of the LGBTQI+ community on Ukrainian soil, which stretches back to antiquity. Our enduring contributions to cultural growth and our commitment to fighting for liberation cannot be ignored.

Recent years have seen the emergence of Ukrainian Queer theory, and we urge readers to get hold of Anton Shebetko's *A Very Brief and Subjective Queer History of Ukraine* and Nataliya Gurba's *Queer Joy, Ukrainian Liberation*. Much like anywhere else, the LGBTQI+ community in Ukraine is far from being a homogeneous entity, and engaging with a vast array of diverse perspectives is vital for developing a nuanced understanding of our past and present.

This anthology is not only a platform for sharing our experiences, it is an archive of our existence and a testament to our permanence. We hope it will contribute to the visibility of queer Ukrainians and inspire more works like it to be produced in the coming years. It's time for us to tell our stories on our own terms – and for you, dear reader, to listen and stand in solidarity with us.

– DViJKA

About DViJKA and Rebel Queers

The DViJKA collective consists of a Kyiv-born, London-based duo of artist-researchers working in the fields of performance, film, writing and archiving. Their work revolves around spotlighting the experiences of LGBTQI+ Ukrainians and documenting the history of queerness on their land.

Rebel Queers is a group of queer activists who work to reclaim their right to the city of Kyiv. Their protests do not define themselves as being against anything, but rather honouring queer people and realising their liberation. Their actions are conscious of transphobia and queerphobia, and how they intersect with other forms of oppression.

QUEER
UKRAINE

AN ANTHOLOGY OF LGBTQi+
UKRAINIAN VOICES DURING WARTIME

MAKSYM ERISTAVI

Ukrainian Queerness

Before drafting this essay, I chatted with a passionate western volunteer who has been helping Ukrainians. The person was frustrated that their family wouldn't understand or share their enthusiasm, but said that finding support within the 'chosen family' of Ukrainians is uplifting.

As a queer Ukrainian, I cannot relate more to the 'chosen family' experience – it is remarkable how this sentiment has become part of the anti-colonial solidarity around Ukraine. It is no coincidence – it was easier for me to come out as queer than as Ukrainian – but after I did both, only then did the queerness of being Ukrainian become so apparent.

The resistance of it: the resistance to the attempts to erase your identity, gaslight, dehumanise, exploit and dominate you.

The survival of it: forging community links in your darkest hour, nurturing the sense of collective care and responsibility for each other, and reclaiming the language and culture codes that were used to oppress you.

The love of it: harbouring faith and hope despite facing the most unspeakable evil humanity is capable of; dreaming and envisioning a world that is more just; preserving devotion to the idea of equality and freedom and liberty; relentlessly trying to reject hate; not losing your ability to love.

These qualities are not only quintessentially queer, but also very anti-colonial.

I want to take a moment during the genocide that my people are enduring to reflect on the colonial nature of homophobia under Russian colonial rule, the everyday manifestation of it, and how the Ukrainian decolonisation struggle is fundamentally queer, because I am sure it is integral to understanding today's Ukrainians' fight, too.

If you knew me as a kid, you would not be surprised to learn that I was more ashamed of coming across as Ukrainian than as gay. I was bullied for my queerness and femininity; but my father's very Ukrainian surname and my Ukrainian accent got me into much more trouble, and I started using my mother's maiden name as an alias.

Growing up in Eastern Ukraine in the 1990s, homophobia was part of my everyday experience, but I'd say this was less a conscious choice to dehumanise and oppress people, and more a lack of education. Moreover, back then, queer acceptance was on the rise across former Russian colonies in Eastern Europe. Belarus[1] and Moldova[2] hosted their first

---

1 Izabelė Švaraitė, 'Minsk Replaced Its Pride Parade with a Festival – and it Worked', LGL: National LGBT Rights Organization (17 December 2017). https://www.lgl.lt/en/?p=19308

2 'Lesbian and Gay Moldova', *Gay Times* (2006). https://web.archive.org/web/20060929204304/http://www.gaytimes.co.uk/gt/listings.asp?action=ShowCountry&CID=656

pride marches in 1999 and 2002 respectively – way ahead of some eastern EU States. Public displays of queerness in pop culture was growing. I might have been called homophobic names in school, but they would always have something to do with the names of prominent queer celebrities of the time.

Things started to roll back in the late 2000s when Russia got its colonial shit together and made the articulated ideology of homophobia part of its neighbourhood foreign policy in the renewed push for colonial domination. This is when Moscow integrated homophobia into a coherent 'civilisation ideology' of Russkiy Mir[1] and provided their neighbourhood proxies with rigorous and appealing talking points about why homophobia (and the repression of women or anything progressive or indigenous) is a superior worldview.[2] The concept that sexual or gender diversity is an 'alien Western concept' is now a strengthening ideology binding millions from Russia to the US and from Brazil to Uganda. It has its roots in the Russian disinformation campaigns[3] of the late 2000s, with the 'Gayrope' concept portraying homosexuality as a Western conspiracy to undermine Vladimir Putin as a self-proclaimed defender

1 Hybrid Warfare Analytical Group, 'Russkiy Mir' as the Kremlin's Quasi-Ideology', *Ukraine Crisis Media Center* (28 May 2021).
https://uacrisis.org/en/russkiy-mir-as-the-kremlin-s-quasi-ideology
2 Alexandra Novitskaya, 'Sexual Citizens in Exile: State-Sponsored Homophobia and Post-Soviet LGBTQI+ Migration', *The Russian Review*, 80:1 (13 January 2021).
https://doi.org/10.1111/russ.12298
3 Maxim Eristavi, 'The 4 Lessons Eastern Europe Teaches Us about Tectonic Shifts at Global LGBT+ Frontlines', *Hebbel Am Ufer* (2019).
https://www.hebbel-am-ufer.de/en/hau3000/four-lessons-maxim-eristavi/

of conservative moral values. The narrative is designed to help Putin to justify neocolonial expansion into neighbouring countries and to preserve regional kleptocracies under the facade of protecting 'a civilisational block'. One of the most prominent features was the export of Russian 'gay propaganda' laws,[1] the adoption of which would be a must to secure financial and political backing from the metropole.

Luckily for queer Ukrainians like me, almost two dozen attempts to pass similar laws in Ukraine all failed. It was no coincidence that they were all initiated and backed by pro-Russian political forces: since the early 2010s institutionalised homophobia quickly became synonymous with the resurgent Russian colonial influence in Ukraine and beyond. You can map pro-Russian political agents in the region[2] by their support for the criminalisation of queerness, even if they would be cautious about publicly identifying as pro-Russian.

I would never have connected the dots between my queerness, my Ukrainianness and Russian colonialism so obviously until something happened to me personally. For almost a year in the early 2010s, I lived in Moscow. It remains the most degrading and revolting experience of my life. I faced virulent homophobia for being openly

---

[1] The Russian Federation, 'The Federal Law for the Purpose of Protecting Children from Information Advocating a Denial of Traditional Family Values' (2013).

[2] Alison Mutler, 'First Russia, Then Hungary, Now Romania Is Considering a "Gay Propaganda" Law', *Radio Free Europe/Radio Liberty* (26 June 2022).
https://www.rferl.org/a/romania-lgbtq-rights-bill-gay-propaganda-law/31915661.html

queer; I faced rabid xenophobia for being Ukrainian; and I faced nasty racism for being mixed-race. I could never tell what it was that provoked specific slurs from random people in the street or micro-aggression at work: my femininity, my Georgian nose, my Asian eyelid fold, my dark Roma hair or my Ukrainian accent. It was too much queerness for folks at the heart of a patriarchal colonial empire to handle.

The coloniality of attempts to criminalise queerness is, of course, not new; it is just the Russian chapter in this history that is rarely acknowledged. As my co-authors and I explain in *Untapped Power*,[1] a book about decolonising our foreign policies to promote more diversity, most laws still existing in former colonies worldwide were first introduced by colonisers.[2] For example, the British colonial empire left a vast trail of anti-sodomy laws in its wake.[3] Russian colonialism was no different: absolutely all anti-homosexuality legislation in former Russian colonies was written in Moscow. To date, the only two surviving laws criminalising homosexuality in the Russian neighbourhood, in Uzbekistan and Turkmenistan, were introduced by the Russian colonial administration in the nineteenth century, and were updated in 1926 during the Soviet colonial occupation.

---

1 Carla Koppell (ed.), *Untapped Power: Leveraging Diversity and Inclusion for Conflict and Development* (New York: Oxford University Press, 2022).

2 Human Rights Watch, 'This Alien Legacy: The Origins of "Sodomy" Laws in British Colonialism' (17 December 2008). https://www.hrw.org/report/2008/12/17/alien-legacy/ origins-sodomy-laws-british-colonialism

3 Dan Healey, *Homosexual Desire in Revolutionary Russia: The Regulation of Sexual and Gender Dissent* (Chicago: The University of Chicago Press, 2001).

Like other Russian colonies, formal attempts to criminalise, marginalise or erase Ukrainian queerness all trace back to times of Russian rule. Traditionally matriarchal, Ukrainian society was historically more comfortable with expressions of femininity, sexual and gender diversity. Long before Russia existed as a unified State, Ukrainian letopises of the Kievan Rus' were freely documenting and glorifying stories of same-sex affection and love.[1]

Take the eleventh-century story of princelings Borys and Gleb,[2] which also documents a deep and possibly romantic affection between Borys and a male friend. Centuries later, Russian colonial rule started systemically erasing any traces of Ukrainian diversity and queerness. That's how, for example, a strict celibacy rule covering any type of sexual acts at military posts of Ukrainian Cossacks turned into a Moscow-pushed myth of an exclusive ban on gay sex by the founders of the first Ukrainian democracy of the seventeenth century (the same historical distortion was also used to erase the prominent role of Ukrainian women during the Cossack era).[3]

Or take the unapologetic and anti-colonial queerness of the Ukrainian literary geniuses Lesya Ukrainka[4] and Taras

---

1 See also p. 43.

2 Nestor the Chronicler, *Lives of Boris and Gleb* (11th century).

3 Oleksandr Kryvoshyj, *Henderni vyklyky frontovoji povsyakdenosti kozats'koho Zaporojya u naukovomu dorobku ukrajins'kyh istoykiv (1946–1991 rr)* (*Gendered Challenges at the Front of Everyday Life of the Cossack Zaporozhye in the Scientific Work of Ukrainian Historians (1946–1991)* (Kyiv: Ukrainoznavchyj Almanah, 2013).

4 Maksym Eristavi and Val Voshchevska, '#UkrainianSpaces: Culture and Feminism', *Ukrainian Spaces* (2022).
https://podcasts.apple.com/us/podcast/
ukrainianspaces-2-culture-and-feminism/id1616395167?i=1000556171143

Shevchenko.[1] Queerness so strong that it still speaks powerfully to Ukrainians generations down the line. 'There's the power in her way of naming herself,' writes Nataliya Gurba in their series of powerful essays[2] on the nexus of queer joy and Ukrainian liberation. 'A new first name. A new last name. What is more queer than that? Weaving her own identity into her community, a full and personal dedication to collective emancipation and liberation.' Colonisers couldn't just erase those voices – their art is intertwined with Ukrainian identity – so they sanitised their legacy to infantile, primitive and heteronormative representations that were fed back to colonised Ukrainians for generations. 'Did she know her softness would be misrepresented, edited in histories into powerlessness? Into naïveté, childishness and sweet meekness? If she did, I think she would be unbothered, and carry on raging and existing against the grain,' Gurba concludes, in a streak of defiance that is both classically queer and Ukrainian.

This queer erasure was only exacerbated during the Soviet era. Take Sergei Parajanov, the prominent Ukrainian director, one of the greatest filmmakers in human history. Unapologetically queer and no less unapologetically Ukrainian, he was bullied and persecuted by the Kremlin most of his life, and you can't be sure whether Parajanov was targeted for his queerness or his anti-colonial art – or both. Russian colonial rulers would

---

1 Alex Fisher, 'From DIK Fagazine to "Was Taras Shevchenko Gay?" Karol Radziszeswki Pursues Ukrainian Queer Identity Across the Centuries', *Artslooker* (14 January 2021).
https://artslooker.com/en/from-dik-fagazine-to-'was-taras-shevchenko-gay-karol-radziszewski-pursues-ukrainian-queer-identit/
2 Nataliya Gurba, *Queer Joy, Ukrainian Liberation* (Canada, printed by the author, 2022).

use criminalised homosexuality as an excuse to put dissidents on trial; it also put many actual homosexuals in jail, labelling them dissidents. Despite persecuting him, Russia appropriated Parajanov's art, sanitised it of queerness and parades it as an example of 'great Russian art' − not that this is the only example of Ukrainian art being stolen by Russian colonialists.[1]

A patriarchal narrative rewriting and cultural erasure of Ukrainian queerness would go hand in hand with Russian colonial rule forcing anti-queer laws[2] on to indigenous communities with no history of formal criminalisation of same-sex relations. Moscow introduced the first such law in 1716,[3] then in 1846,[4] 1903,[5] 1934[6] and 1961.[7] At the same time,

---

1 See, for example, Potiah Om, 'Ukrainian Artists Appropriated by Russia', Instagram (6 April 2022).
https://www.instagram.com/p/CcA9s65tq1k/
2 *Korotka Istorija Homoseksualnych Represij V Ukrajini* (*A Timeline Outlining the History of Repressions of Homosexuality in Ukraine*) (Kyiv: Pinchuk Art Centre, no date).
https://pinchukartcentre.org/files/img/fgap/files/motta_newspaper_ua.pdf
3 A. Man'kov, *Artykul Voinskij* (*Military Article*) (Russia: Juridicheskaja Literatura, 1986).
4 'Ulozhenije o nakazanijyah ugolovnyx i ispravitelnix 1845 goda' ('Code of Penal and Correctional Punishments of 1845'), *Istorya.ru.*
http://www.istorya.ru/referat/6279/1.php
5 *Novoje ugolovnoje ulozhenije, vys. utv. 22 marta 1903* (*New Criminal Code of 22 March 1905*) (St Petersburg: Book. Mag. V.P. Anisimova, 1903).
https://viewer.rusneb.ru/ru/000199_000009_003714958
6 Centralny Vykonavchyj Komitet USSR, 'Centralny Vykonavchyj Komitet UkSSR III Sesjia XIII Sklykan'ya' ('Central Executive Committee of the USSR III Session XIII Convocation'), *Liga 360* (2022).
https://ips.ligazakon.net/document/KP360002?an=2
7 Verhovna Rada Ukrainy, 'Kriminalnij Kodex Ukrainy' ('Ukraine Criminal Codex'), *Verhovna Rada Ukrainy* (26 January 2011).
https://zakon.rada.gov.ua/laws/show/2001-05/ed19911212#top

there were systemic colonial attempts to erase the Ukrainian language and culture[1] (not to mention Ukrainians in general, with the Holodomor genocide)[2] over the same period.

To Russian colonialists, Ukrainianness and Queerness are two equally criminal and dangerous acts of existence. It is not surprising that the rapid expansion of human rights equality and queer visibility in Ukraine coincided with a broad decolonial awakening.

With symbolism that is no coincidence, it started with a cultural rebellion against colonial patriarchal norms. From the late 1980s, the trailblazing Ukrainian writer Oksana Zabuzhko penned brilliantly woven manifestos reclaiming her body, her sexuality and her rights, with fearless and visionary exposure of Russian rule in Ukraine. Then, in the early 2000s, the visionary camp artist Andriy Danylko channelled cheekily masked anti-colonial satire through the quintessentially queer character Verka Serduchka. Danylko's stand-up performances were littered with clichés about Ukrainian inferiority, which he then reclaimed, and built back Ukrainian national pride – all through humour, through the art of camp. He took Russian audiences by storm – they loved the portrayals of Ukrainians as funny, feisty simpletons, and failed to realise that their applause, devoid of any self-reflection or self-irony, formed the final act of this brilliant anti-colonial art. Publicly resisting Russian

---

1 'Zaborona ukrayinskoyi movy' ('Prohibition of the Ukrainian Language'), *Encyclopedia of Modern Ukraine* (Kyiv: NASU Institute of Encyclopedic Research, 2020).
https://esu.com.ua/search_articles.php?id=17240
2 'About' (Kyiv: National Museum of the Holodomor-Genocide, 2022).
https://holodomormuseum.org.ua/en/

attempts to appropriate his art, Danylko was banished from Moscow at the same time as Verka Serduchka took the queer world by storm with the cheeky wordplay in the Eurovision hit 'Dancing Lasha Tumbai' (largely interpreted to mean 'Russia, goodbye').[1] It is perhaps unsurprising, then, that during the ongoing genocide the early stand-up performances of Verka Serduchka are proving to be powerful anti-colonial art that helps to keep spirits high.

In 2014 the Maidan Revolution brought another powerful anti-colonial jolt for Ukrainian society when Kremlin attempts to solidify colonial control over the country and rob us of the right to rejoin the European family were resisted. With this jolt came larger queer acceptance, because queer people would fight and die shoulder to shoulder with the rest for freedom of speech, peaceful assembly and self-determination.[2] In the following years, that helped to turbo-charge queer visibility in Ukraine,[3] and the public started to see virulent homophobia as an integral part of Russian influence over the country.

The political earthquake of 2019, when Ukrainians voted in the youngest and most progressive leadership we've ever

---

1 Verka Serduchka, 'Verka Serduchka – Dancing Lasha Tumbai (Ukraine) 2007 Eurovision Song Contest', YouTube (12 January 2012). https://www.youtube.com/watch?v=hfjHJneVonE

2 Ian Daniel, 'Discussing LGBTQ Equality with One of Ukraine's Only Openly Gay Journalists', *Vice* (8 September 2016). https://www.vice.com/en/article/bn3mgq/ discussing-lgbtq-equality-with-one-of-the-ukraines-only-openly-gay-journalists

3 Matthew Mpoke Bigg, 'LGBTQ Activists in Ukraine Share the Fight Against Russia's Invasion', *The New York Times* (17 March 2022). https://www.nytimes.com/2022/03/17/world/russia-ukraine-queer-activists. html

seen, also helped. Before taking office as the leader of the country, President Zelenskyy wasn't a stranger to passionate defence of what's right – like dignity for queer Ukrainians.[1]

But the real game changer for queer equality in Ukraine came on the 24th of February 2022, with the genocide launched by Russia. Queer Ukrainians were among the first to enlist to defend the country – they knew all too well that there was more at stake than territorial integrity. It was the ultimate civilisational battle for Ukraine, paved by centuries of anti-colonial struggle. If this war is lost, queerness and Ukrainianness will be buried in the same mass grave.

That's why now we have tens of thousands of openly queer soldiers proudly and visibly[2] defending Ukraine and the rest of Europe from Russian colonial fascism. That's why a public petition for marriage equality, addressed to the President, collected the minimum requirement of 25,000 signatures in no time.[3] That's why our officials are meeting queer activists to work on effective hate-crime legislation while bombs literally rain down over their heads.[4] That's

---

1 Maksym Eristavi, 'That viral video of Ukraine's President @ZelenskyyUa powerfully shutting down a homophobic heckler – now with more context by @Hromadske. A rare public exhibit of passion in defending progressive values by a European leader these days', *Twitter* (13 October 2019).
https://twitter.com/maksymeristavi/status/1183405321970163713?lang=en
2 https://lgbtmilitary.org.ua/eng.
3 Sophie Williams, 'Ukraine to Consider Legalising Same-Sex Marriage Amid War', BBC News (12 July 2022).
https://www.bbc.co.uk/news/world-europe-62134804
4 KyivPride, 'Homophobic and Transphobic Crimes in Ukraine During Wartime Should Be Investigated!', *KyivPride* (14 June 2022).
https://www.facebook.com/kyivpride/posts/pfbid02ikbYFAkQzUCCAZyS-rCJ8zmhFTmBNDk5NHU8zHBTHZ9femZiKyKKC5DSBbpjV7veel

why public acceptance of queer Ukrainians reached all-time highs of 64% during the war.[1]

I spoke to another queer Ukrainian storyteller, Maria,[2] also known as Vinok Collective,[3] who told me, 'Folks are starting to understand that we are fighting for Ukrainian identity, for Ukrainian pride, for a Ukrainian future and for the Ukrainian right to exist. And queer Ukrainians really, truly understand this on such an intimate level because we have already had to fight these battles. We've already had to fight for the right to exist, wherever we are – whether in Ukraine or Canada, or wherever we are. We've had to fight to exist, be recognised and be acknowledged. We've had to fight for pride. And this is what all of Ukraine is doing right now. So [queerness and Ukrainianness are] very intimately intertwined, and I think the average person is starting to get a lot of clarity on this.'

So it is no coincidence that queer acceptance and decolonisation go hand in hand in Ukraine – they are intertwined within the ultimate queerness of being a Ukrainian – but a long journey still lies ahead for both challenges.

---

1 Markiyan Klymkovetskyi, 'V Ukrajini vdvichi zrosla pidtrymka rivnyx prav dlya LGBT za ostani roky – opytuvan'ya KMIS' ('In Ukraine Support for Equal Rights for LGBT People has doubled in Recent Years – KMIS Survey', *Hromadske* (1 June 2022).
https://hromadske.ua/posts/v-ukrayini-vdvichi-zrosla-pidtrimka-rivnih-prav-dlya-lgbt-za-ostanni-roki-opituvannya-kmis
2 Maksym Eristavi and Val Voshchevska, '#UkrainianSpaces: The Queerness of Being a Ukrainian', *Ukrainian Spaces* (2022).
https://podcasts.apple.com/us/podcast/
ukrainianspaces-23-the-queerness-of-being-a-ukrainian/
id1616395167?i=1000570627146
3 https://www.instagram.com/vinokcollective/.

Back in 2015, I wrote an essay that, in many ways, defined my public image for many years after. Entitled 'I'm Gay in Ukraine and My Country Despises Me',[1] it was an honest message of frustration and anger of a young queer person who is denied an equal claim to humanity and dignity every day. But it was also an honest message from a confused mind that wasn't touched by the enlightenment of decolonisation; that anger and despair were valid, but misdirected. It took me years to see that the fastest shortcut to equality in Ukraine is decolonial awakening.[2] This awakening builds a mental bridge between two very similar experiences: being queer and being Ukrainian. Both are surviving, resisting and prevailing, despite centuries of oppression by Russian colonialism.

---

1 Maxim Eristavi, 'I'm Gay in Ukraine and my Country Despises Me', *Politico* (27 November 2015).

https://www.politico.eu/article/gay-ukraine-my-country-despises-me/

2 Joey Harvey, 'Not Even Russian Bombs Can Silence Queer Ukrainian Journalist Maksym Eristavi', *Queerty* (26 May 2022).

https://www.queerty.com/not-even-russian-bombs-can-silence-queer-ukraini-an-journalist-maksym-eristavi-20220526

MARICHKA

even if you run from the war, it will remain in your insides
anxiety shut herself off behind ten locks in the corner of my mind
glued the windows shut with criss-crossed tape, left documents in
    my pockets
she runs through corridors and screams of mercurial moments
doesn't like to walk the dog in the evenings (though she'd longed for
    summer all winter)
she sees disgusting, nonsensically realistic dreams when she's sleeping
she waits for the wailing of sirens, waits for exhaustion and commotion
on the twenty-fourth at six a.m. my roots were cut off in motion
i invite my anxiety for coffee, tell her we've finally found safety
but anxiety doesn't believe me, for what dwells in my heart is bloody

YANA LYS (LYSHKA)

Transness in Traditional Ukrainian Culture

The LGBTQI+ movement in Ukraine is subject to plenty of stereotypes. A popular line, propagated by authoritarian socio-political powers, portrays the LGBTQI+ community as a 'folly imposed on Ukraine by the liberal democracy of the West'.

This rhetoric is poorly masked, and can be traced back to the Soviet and Putinist tradition, when the totalitarian propaganda started adding the adjective 'rotting'/'rotten' to the noun 'West'.

So, transness and LGBTQI+ identities are looked at not as a multifaceted phenomenon, but as an 'unhealthy folly', born in the democratic, free, but 'depraved' western culture. In Soviet times expressions such as 'the bourgeois overate, so they've gone mad from all the fat' proliferated, outlining plenty of cultural differences.

The entrenchment of this stereotype in the collective subconscious, preserved by the authority of the traditionalist wing of the scientific community, severely slows down – if not fully freezes – cultural studies of Ukraine's LGBTQI+ history, especially in historical terms.

Of course, there is no official ban on queerness, since Ukraine has certain obligations to fulfil as part of its process towards EU integration. However, the unspoken taboo on queer studies has blocked the recognition of the primordiality or traditions of LGBTQI+ people on Ukrainian land.

After all, if, against material evidence, people continue to affirm that 'back in the day we did not have this', then the LGBTQI+ community as a whole – and trans folks in particular – are, from a conservative point of view, a new cultural perversion.

With the help of publicly available sources, this essay takes a look at transness in Ukrainian traditional culture. Was it there all along? Was it depicted in ancient myths and social relations? Or did we 'not have this' until the end of the twentieth century?

The list of resources in this text is only intended to serve as a guide, and by searching online for additional information on the facts presented in this text, one can find a multitude of articles, books and internet discussions. But isn't that precisely the point – in order to see the picture in a stained-glass window, one looks at the whole picture from a distance, rather than looking closely at each and every separate piece of glass.

So let's broaden our focus from the fragmented to the whole and venture into the depths of the past.

Antiquity

TRANSNESS IN GREEK MYTHOLOGY

A new epoch began with the arrival of a people on Ukrainian land – the Greeks. They established their colonies on the Ukrainian shores of the Black Sea in around the seventh century BC. In this era, the biggest Greek towns were Tyras (now Bilhorod-Dnistrovskyi), Olbia (near Mykolaiv), Chersonesus (on the outskirts of present-day Sevastopol), Panticapaeum (now Kerch).

Skilled at literacy and communication, the Greeks not only actively traded with the local population, but also intermixed with it. According to the 'father of history', Herodotus (fifth century BC), the Budini (described as a proto-Slavic people) lived in the Left Bank of Ukraine and eagerly accepted Greek immigrants. A stratum of Gelonians – half-Budini and half-Greek – flourished in their society.[1]

Not only did the Greeks influence Slavic culture, but they also took part in the ethnogenesis of proto-Ukrainians. Enough has been said about their influence on the residents of Kievan Rus'. After all, it was the Greeks who brought both Christianity and the Cyrillic alphabet to ancient Ukraine between the ninth and tenth centuries.

---

1 Herodotus, *Book IV: Melpomene, Histories*.

The ancient Greek polytheistic religion had a vast array of myths that explored transness and LGBTQI+ culture as a whole, and myths can be seen as an expression of societal attitudes towards different aspects of life.

For example, representations of the goddess of love and beauty, Aphrodite, vary in terms of gender, and in Cyprus statues of 'Aphroditus' were common, depicting the aforementioned goddess in feminine clothing, but with a beard, or as a woman with male genitalia.

Representations of the god of nature, Dionysus, also challenge gender norms. At times, he was depicted in a nymph dress made of fox fur, wearing other articles of 'feminine' clothing.

Alongside tales of liaisons with many beautiful women, Dionysus also loved Ganymede, a feminine boy, whom he made a cupbearer on Mount Olympus. (Those born under the star sign of Aquarius may find it interesting that Ganymede and Aquarius are one and the same.)

Dionysus's father, Zeus, is portrayed as having breasts in one of his many portrayals (Zeus Labraundos), as is Hermes, in some later representations, and Hermaphroditus, the son of Hermes and Aphrodite, was simultaneously a man and a woman.[1]

Androgyny was often seen as the image of primordial harmony. According to the ancient Greek philosopher Plato, the first people on earth were androgynous, but the gods grew jealous, and split them into two sexes so that humanity would become weak and unable to compete with them.[2]

---

[1] Hans Licht, *Sexual Life in Ancient Greece*, trans. by J.H. Freese (London: Routledge, 1931).

[2] Plato, *The Symposium*.

The idea of androgyny as an ideal state of divine being is not limited to Greek mythology – neither the angels in Christian iconography nor the Bodhisattva in Buddhist iconography possess vividly expressed gender characteristics – in fact, Bodhisattva Avalokiteśvara is depicted as both man and woman.[1]

The impact Greek painting had on late Christian iconography is widely known, but, you may ask, how does Buddhism factor into it? In fact, the canonical Mahayana Buddhist iconography was created under the influence of Greek art after the arrival of Alexander the Great's troops to India in the fourth century BC.

And Greek mythology relating to transness was not limited to tales of the gods – indeed, there are several similar stories about teenage girls who begged the gods to make them male. In each case, the gods are said to have heard their prayers and transformed them into men – Iphis, Caeneus and Leucippe. 'For in the name of truth, Iphis, who was a girl, is now a man!' wrote Ovid.[2] There's also the story of Attis, a beautiful young consort of the goddess Cybele, who performed gender-affirming surgery on himself and became a female servant of Cybel, as later popularised by the Roman poet Catullus.[3]

So it seems that the ancient Greeks were tolerant towards diverse gender and sexual self-expression – not only in myth, but in daily life.

---

1 Yulia I. Elikhina, 'Buddhist Sculptures which Belonged to Academician F.I. Stcherbatsky', *Tibetology in St Petersburg: Collected Papers, Issue 1* (St Petersburg: St Petersburg Centre for Oriental Studies Publishers, 2014).
2 Ovid, *Metamorphoses*, Book IX, trans. Brookes More (Boston: Cornhill Publishing Co., 1922).
3 Catullus, 'Attis', *Carmina* 63.

TRANSGENDER SOOTHSAYERS AND

SCYTHIAN WARRIORS

Everything is relatively clear with the Greeks. However, the origins of Ukrainian culture are commonly traced back to the Scythians[1] – which doesn't come as a surprise, since during the Middle Ages our lands were sometimes called the Great Scythia.

As with the Greeks, Scythians first appeared on Ukrainian territory in the seventh century BC – although the word 'appeared' is not quite appropriate here, as 'Scythian' isn't a purely ethnic concept, but rather an ethnocultural label, and as such there were Iranian-speaking royal and nomadic Scythians (in Crimea and the coast of the Black Sea), as well as Scythian farmers (in Central Ukraine), who are thought to be Proto-Slavic people.[2]

The militancy of the Scythians – especially their scalping of their enemies – was immortalised in the arts, and is still eagerly glorified by the supporters of the military-conservative development in Ukraine. Yet this overlooks and obscures other cultural traditions – their love of cannabis smoke, as described by Herodotus,[3] or their acceptance of transgender people.

In Scythian culture, trans women played an important role in society as priests, or soothsayers, known as the Enarei (from the Iranian *anarya*, or 'unmanly').

---

1 We won't discuss the ancient matriarchal Tripolye culture, with its statues with breasts and serpent ornaments, as written sources are few and far between.

2 Douglas Q Adams, *Encyclopedia of Indo-European Culture* (London and Chicago: Fitzroy Dearborn, 1997).

3 See p. 29.

As previously mentioned, belonging to the aristocracy allowed transgender people, even in the nineteenth century, to be themselves.

The most famous example of this on Ukrainian soil in the New Age is Nadiya (Nadezhda) Durova, also known as Oleksandr Oleksandrov, a more modern-day Joan of Arc.

She was born in 1783 in Kyiv, to retired hussar officer Andriy Durov, from the noble Cossack family of Turovsky and Marfa Durova (Oleksandrovych), the daughter of a Poltava landowner. At eighteen years old, Nadiya was wed against her will to Vasiliy Chernov. After giving birth to a son, Ivan, she left her husband and returned to her parents with the child.[1]

In 1806, she left home, taking an old set of men's Cossack clothes with her and assuming the identity of a landowner's son, Oleksandr Durov.[2] In this identity he joined the Don Cossack regiment, which was on its way to fight the French. He was accepted by a comrade (a member of the nobility) of the Polish Cavalry Regiment under the name Oleksandr Sokolov. Over the next year, he took part in battles against the French in Europe, receiving an award for bravery.

In 1807, he wrote to inform his family of his whereabouts. His father immediately demanded his return, and

---

1 V.A. Smoliy (ed.), 'Durova', *Encyclopedia of the History of Ukraine*, 2 (Kyiv: National Academy of Sciences of Ukraine, 2004).

2 Dmitri Mendeleev and Vladimir Solovyov (eds.), 'Durova', *The Brockhaus and Efron Encyclopedic Dictionary*, XI (1893), pp. 247–48.

Oleksandr was sent to St Petersburg to meet the emperor, Tsar Alexander I, who wanted to take a look at the so-called 'maiden-cavalryman'.

The unthinkable happened: the charismatic Oleksandr so impressed the tsar that he was granted independence from his father. The emperor, recognising the 'maiden-cavalryman' as a new Amazon, further decreed he be transferred to the Mariupol regiment, stationed in Volyn and the Ternopyl region, where, for a time, he served as aide-de-camp to the General and Military Governor of Kyiv, Mikhaylo Myloradovych.

In 1812, during the war against Napoleon, Oleksandr sustained an injury, and spent a stint as an adjutant to Field Marshal Mikhaylo Kutuzov himself. In 1816, he retired from his position as chief of staff.

He wrote a memoir about his experiences, entitled *Notes of a Calvary Maiden* (1836), which was regarded highly by Alexander Pushkin. In the book, Oleksandr described his self-identification, saying: 'two emotions, in such direct opposition – my love for my father and my repulsion for my sex – perturbed my young soul with an equal force, and I, with a firmness and endurance uncharacteristic of my age, began to contemplate the plan to abandon the sphere designated to me by nature and by the customs of the female sex.'

When his son sent a letter seeking his blessing to be wed, addressing Oleksandr as 'Mother', he threw the letter into the fireplace without bothering to read it. Only after another letter arrived, addressed to Oleksandr Andriyovich, did he reply with a blessing.

Judging by these anecdotes it seems fair to say that Oleksandr wasn't only gender-nonconforming, but was probably transgender. In the Soviet era he was, of course, exclusively portrayed as being a brave woman; likewise, this stance is taken in Eldar Ryazanov's cute but historically inaccurate film about Durov, *Hussar's Ballad* (1962).

Oleksandr died in 1866 in Yelabuz, Vyatka Province (now Tatarstan). He asked to be remembered as 'Oleksandr, God's servant', but the priest refused to part with the Church's rules. He was awarded military honours at the burial.

In addition to the Kyiv native, Tetyana Markina, from the village of Natavska on the banks of the river Don, had a similar journey in the Russian Empire even earlier. She, too, joined the army, in which she fought for quite a long time as the Cossack Kurtochkin. Additionally (already as an officer), he fought in western Ukraine in 1792 in the ranks of the Russian Imperial army against the Polish army.

His identity was exposed during that year, and he met with Empress Yekaterina II, who forbade him to continue military service under a male name, so he returned to his village, where, in 1793, he took part in an uprising of the Cossacks against their forced displacement to the Kuban. The uprising was successful, and they retained their right to live on their land. Kurtochkin died in his native village, and was buried in a military uniform.[1]

---

1 Laurie Stoff, *They Fought for the Motherland Russia's Women Soldiers in World War I and the Revolution* (Kansas: University Press of Kansas, 2006).

Modern Times

(UP TO THE MID-TWENTIETH CENTURY)

TRANSGENDER PEOPLE IN THE USSR

In Ukraine, the beginning of the twentieth century came not with the achievement of democracy, as was the case in the West, but with totalitarian regimes: Russo-Soviet (1920–41, 1944–91) and German national-socialist (1941–44). A 'normal' citizen, brainwashed by Soviet propaganda could say: 'At last, they've definitely got rid of transgender people in Ukraine!'

Trans people were almost completely eradicated – at least until the end of the 1980s, which brought with it Mikhail Gorbachev's failed Perestroika – almost nowhere to be seen, portrayed as a cultural infection, with a very few marginalised exceptions.

The beginning of the Soviet erasure of trans people is rooted in the last year of the revolution, when arrests made by the Soviet police of '95 men, partly disguised as women' at 6 Simeonivska Street, Petrograd, on the 15th of January, 1921, gained widespread attention.[1] It was an illegal party of St Petersburg's transgender population, and one can safely assume that there were Ukrainians present – after all, it was the ex-capital (until 1918), where many representatives of all the peoples of Russian Empire resided.

---

1 Stephen Amico, 'Gay-Made Space' in *Roll Over, Tchaikovsky! Russian Popular Music and Post-Soviet Homosexuality* (Illinois: University of Illinois Press, 2014), pp. 135–66.

Criminal cases were swiftly opened, and the fact that there were military members present among the convicted caused an uproar. While only those present at the ill-fated party were arrested, according to the reports of the undercover agent responsible for the arrests, Afanasy Shaur, the trans community in St Petersburg numbered over 2,000 people – although the police weren't necessarily good at differentiating transgender people from other members of the LGBTQI+ community, so there are arguments for adjusting the number quoted both up and down.

Those arrested were relatively lucky (these weren't Stalinist times yet, but the 'softer' years under the rule of Lenin), and, in 1922, the convicted were diagnosed as mentally ill (by none other than the neurologist and psychologist Vladimir Bekhterev), but were not subjected to treatment.

A sceptic might object that perhaps there were Ukrainians amongst those people, but perhaps there weren't, and overall this is a discussion about Soviet-era Russia rather than Soviet-era Ukraine. But we have no data about such large-scale events taking place in, say, Kyiv or Kharkiv.

There was another scandal in 1972, in Soviet-era Lithuania, when Soviet surgeon Viktor Kalnberz performed the first genital-correction operation in the USSR.

Of course, he was punished. He wasn't thrown behind bars, but was given a stern reprimand for 'performing an operation that cripples the individual and does not correspond to the order and ideology of the state'. Furthermore, a member of the commission that reviewed the surgeon's actions offered a counterargument to Kalnberz's claim that the patient was on the verge of suicide due to the disconnect between their primary sex characteristics and their gender identity: 'What foolishness! Should've let her kill herself!'[1]

It seems transgender and nonconforming Ukrainians (those who weren't arrested under Stalin or slaughtered during the Holodomor) were in hiding – but, statistically speaking, they must have still existed, and in all spheres of society, unless you consider lack of evidence to be proof of the reverse.

Postscript

As we have seen, in the twentieth century transgender people did not disappear.

There's a problematic mentality that prohibits us from seeing real, living people in prominent Ukrainian historical figures. Rarely might one read about, for instance, the Chief Otaman of the Ukrainian People's Republic Symon Petliura being a Freemason, and in 1919 becoming the Grand Master of the Grand Lodge of Ukraine,[2] or about the head of the Directorate of the National People's Republic of Ukraine, Volodymyr Vynnychenko, being a staunch vegetarian and a founding philosopher of Concordism; but talking about

---

[1] Anton Smirnov, 'Pervaya zavershennaya operatsiya po smene pola, Riga, 1972 god' ('The First Completed Gender Reassignment Surgery. Riga, 1972' *Medportal* (18 June 2020).

https://medportal.ru/enc/plasurgery/reading/57/

[2] Viktor Savchenko, 'Masonstvo v Ukraine v XX veke' ('Freemasonry in Ukraine in the Twntieth Century'), Freemason.org.ua (no date). https://www.freemason.org.ua/uk-UA/Masonstvo-v-Ukraini/Masonstvo-v-Ukrayne-v-HH-veke.aspx?ID=19

people's gender nonconformance or sexuality? No, no, no! You can't include such things in history books!

Having explored history and found a few cases, let's return to the question posed at the beginning of this essay: Is transness a modern phenomenon?

No. As we have seen, it has always existed on Ukrainian soil, for the very simple reason that transgender people have existed in all eras, in all societies, since the dawn of time.

When modern authoritarian-conservative socio-political forces call for restrictions on the rights of the LGBTQI+ community, saying it 'does not correspond to traditional Ukrainian culture', they're either lying or simply ignorant about our country's history. Their conservatism is akin to the attitudes of the Middle Ages – or worse: to the totalitarian ideologies of the twentieth century. Either way, their attitudes certainly aren't born from 'ancient Ukrainian traditions'.

Why is any of this important? Because an attack on human freedoms always begins with the subjugation of the most vulnerable communities. Once you strip away the rights of sexual and gender minorities, then national, religious and social minorities, these people will be driven into ghettos. After that, various 'socially useless' people follow – artists, scientists and, of course, women ('children, kitchen, church – and that's enough for them!'). And not long after, the average representative of the 'right' majority will eventually discover that he, too, has been deprived of his freedom.

Perhaps it is only when the majority of Ukrainians cease to see everything in black and white and instead begin to see the world in a full spectrum that we will finally see real change, and be able to build a harmonious, dutiful, tolerant – and therefore truly mature and strong – society. For consciousness also determines being, and not just the other way around.

Quo vadis? Where are you going? You have to ask yourself this question in time…

GOODVAMPIRE

Today I've begun to doubt my life again. It feels as though the war isn't solely fought on the battlefield, but inside my psyche.

On a daily basis I consume more information, upon which my life depends, neurotically absorbing every detail.

Another air raid alert spent in the restroom – right now, that's the safest place. My parents are driving me mad – they haven't learned to control their emotions. When our lives were turned upside down, did we somehow switch roles? Why don't I feel the war that's happening in front of my very eyes as fiercely? Am I used to it? Perhaps this isn't new any more.

Stress. Loneliness. Stress. Everything's all right with me. Stress. Society. Study and forewarn. Solve and rationalise. Stress. My life.

It has become a joke: why bother planning something for the upcoming month if a rocket might kill you in the next hour?

Death is the last thing that scares me right now. It's more difficult to understand the incomprehensibility and hollowness of what I once called 'the future'.

I'm grateful for the childhood traumas that prepared me for the inhumanity and paradoxes of war.

'Free in thought, but closed in my actions.' Are these my words? Is this something from my creative work or an observation of the alteration of my consciousness?

The search for a mental disorder – is it an attempt to find a justification for my imperfections, or indicative of depression?

Is the fact that I haven't formed any close relationships and that I'm terribly affected by a state of profound agitation caused by my past or my present? My future has ceased to exist.

I'm afraid of men – no, not exactly; it's the aggression that scares me, so in avoiding eye contact, I'm hoping to avoid physical or emotional violence. That's why I've entered online spaces. This way I can't see a face, a feeling, but I can project the illusion of real communication on to replicas.

Jealousy, hatred, egocentrism, friendship, sincerity. Where can I find the right words to express my joy for those friends who have the chance and the fortitude to grow during this time?

For how long have we been fighting without being heard?

Eight years, or several months?

For how long have we been fighting for our personal identity?

I've only just begun – but Ukraine: for hundreds of years and millions of lives.

ALSU GARA

1

there will be no space
on the grounds taken through terror
to live out the truth of my love
there will be no space
on the grounds so blood-soaked
to have the freedom to be
who i fought to become
i call out my nen'ko Ukrayina
to pull me back to the grounds
fertile enough to revive me
she sings to me in my sleep
of the blood that has poisoned
her body.
now my identity lies
at the hands of my freedom
bleeding its essence out
on to the holy ukrainian grounds
and my being's too injured
to get up and provide
my nen'ko with her last kiss of goodbye

who will i be if she dies
who will i have to become
where do i find the strength
to live on and find out
i only want to be who i am now
a body made out of freedom
a body born to love and be loved
do not ask me to sacrifice
such a saintly feeling
i am keeping it for my
nen'ko Ukrayina

2

our last kiss on the tip of my sword
our last goodbyes in the barrel of my gun
god knows this fight is centuries old
it ends when our love is revived
i will not let a thing bury my body without
you coming back to it & once again giving it love
there is no other way for me to go down
than in the embrace of the freedom
to choose who we are
to choose who we love
to choose who we are buried beside
let me carry this promise to the heart of this fight
that even if my body is gone
i will keep our love for ever alive

ERNEST HUK

The Emancipation of Ernie

Every single moment following 4 a.m. on the 24th of February is incomprehensible. But it is a moral imperative for Ukrainians in the intellectual (battle)field to reflect on and preserve as many artefacts as possible. For too long, we were fed up with imported narratives on our own history as part of colonisation, either from the East or West, and they have to be immediately eradicated if we are to sustain our sovereignty.

In 2014, more or less as a reaction to the triumph of Euromaidan, Russia occupied Crimea and Donbas and the Russo-Ukrainian war began. At the time, I was a small-town boy from the very west of Ukraine, pursuing his dream to study in the capital and change his country for the better (yes, I'm a *Legally Blonde* fan). My outgoing nature and urge for validation soon led to me getting sucked into Kyiv's simmering hipster economy (*Arma Comes*) *Closer,* Cxema, Podmost, Optimus, *Vogue, UFW, MBKFD,* Pinchuk Art Centre, *Don't Take Fake,* 86 Festival, Plivka, Kyiv School, Gogol Fest, Brave! and so on.

In other words, I became primarily a miserable Russian-speaking snob (although I am from a Ukrainian-speaking family), fetishising Soviet-era modernism (do you still remember the Calvert's New East?) and thus criticising decommunisation. I spent all my money on Russian books – mostly from the publishers Garage and Strelka – mostly consumed news from *Meduza* and *Нож*, listened to podcasts from *Radio Mayak*, studied art on Arzamas, humanities on Syg.ma and sociology on PostNauka. And music (**deep breath**) – Kedr Livansky, Samjoe Bolshoje Prostoje Chislo, Pussy Riot, IC3PEAK, МЫ, Zemfira, Shortparis, Antoha MC, t.A.T.u., Kate NV, Dmitri Shostakovich, Igor Stravinsky… This list can go on and on.

Of course, all of the above was a very small part of what my hipster peers and I were consuming at the time, since most trends were still coming over from the West. But still, it's baffling – until 2014 I was a convinced nationalist, boycotting books and music in Russian on principle.

In 2015 Okean Elzy, arguably the most famous Ukrainian band, released the song 'It's Not Your War' – and the terrifying truth is that it wasn't. We were calling it the 'Anti-Terrorist Operation' or similar, to play it down and erase it from our lives, to keep our comfortable status quo intact so we could go back to drinking matcha undisturbed. Narratives about 'Liberal Russians' were very welcome among us.

My story wouldn't be complete without looking at the adverse effects of importing uncontextualised theoretical frameworks from the West. I have always been attracted to guys, but my ultimate realisation that I was gay happened only when I moved out from my small conservative home town to pursue a sociology degree in Kyiv.

There I was exposed to two clashing forms of gender scholarship, presented by two passionate lecturers: (1) liberal feminist/homonationalist; and (2) intersectional feminist/queer. In classes focusing on the first framework, we were acquainted with gay people living in Ukraine who managed to enjoy their lives and succeed in their careers while being open about their sexual identity (I was shocked). In classes using the second approach, the successes of these same people were criticised based on them being white, male and 'too cis'. In the first, I discovered what 'coming out' is; in the second, I found out what an inherently homophobic practice it is.

This clash was going on not only in this academic context, but also in the Ukrainian LGBTQI+ community.

In 2018 I attended my first Pride in Kyiv. Apart from noticing that there were as many police personnel protecting the march from the reactionary harassers as there were event participants, I was impressed by the presence of two distinct groups in the parade, with opposing slogans. First was the LGBTQ Military, headed by the veteran Viktor Pylypenko in the first rows of the march; next came an Anti-Pride cohort, headed by queer activist Fritz von Klein. Correspondingly, there were two slogans: 'Glory to the Nation! Death to Enemies!' and 'Death to the Nation! Queer to Enemies!' As far as I remember, the second one was more numerous.

I have followed LGBTQ Military, an association of Ukrainian LGBTQI+ military, veterans and volunteers, since its conception after Anton Shebetko's exhibition 'We Were Here' at Izolyatsia in 2018.[1] That year I had to choose my thesis topic and, oh goodness, how badly I wanted to write about those courageous people. Still, I didn't. Firstly, I was scared that it could 'out' me (and coming out is an

1 See https://lgbtmilitary.org.ua.

inherently homophobic practice anyway, remember); secondly, I wasn't confident enough to engage in the clash between homonationalism and its queer critique. Paraphrasing Fritz von Klein, my lecturer asserted, 'What is wrong about being gay and a patriot? Pretty much everything.'

So in the end, the title of my thesis was, *Generational Differentiation in Contemporary Ukrainian Society: Value Measuring* – a shallow paper on a shallow subject I had zero personal attachment to. A true embodiment of contemporary science.

As I write, it is September 2022. I am living as an openly gay person, and I am in my third year of my MA at Charles University in Prague. Next year I'll defend my thesis, which is titled, *Rainbow Kobzar: LGBTQI+ Community in the Ranks of the Armed Forces of Ukraine.* I now consume no Russian content; I will speak Russian under no circumstances; I've never been, and I'll never be to Russia. While we naïvely rooted for 'Liberal Russia', did it enthusiastically root for us?

Meanwhile, my relationship with queer theory and the queer community is much more complicated. Although many crucial issues have been addressed, there is still a long way to go – after all, it is only worth discussing same-sex marriage once you can hold hands in public with your same-sex partner without having your face broken. It makes much more sense to criticise patriotism when you are a patriot of an imperialistic entity; conversely, Ukrainian nationalism is, by definition, anti-colonial. If intersectional scholarship keeps failing to recognise this, it will do more harm to those it aspired to emancipate.

I have no ability to predict what direction western scholarship will take in the foreseeable future. Yet, finishing on a bright note, I am absolutely sure of every invader's destiny whose feet have touched my homeland's soil: They who draw the sword will die by the sword.

OLEKSANDR BOSIVSKI

Family

Sem'ya (*Family*) is a project that reflects upon the heteronormativity of social and cultural perceptions of relationships and connections between people, and the perception of LGBTQI+ individuals within these relationships as 'close friends', 'relatives', 'roommates', etc.

Sem'ya is based on a painting by the queer British painter Gluck (born Hannah Gluckstein), *Medallion* (1936),[1] a portrayal of the artist with her lover, Neta Obermer, reimagined through my current stance as an artist, through a queer-trans lens.

In 1936, Gluck's painting was interpreted by the public, enforced by societal norms, as depicting 'sisters' or 'friends', even though it was a queer depiction of lovers. As such, the queer message of *Medallion* was stripped and made

---

1 Gluck, *Medallion* ('*YouWe*') (1936).
https://www.royalacademy.org.uk/article/
magazine-gluck-brighton-museum-art-gallery-diana-souhami

heterosexual. *Sem'ya*, on the other hand, depicts me and my mother – to some this might come across as a 'hetero' notion of family, but in actual fact it is a queer portrayal, as I'm a non-binary faggot and my mother is asexual.

The painting is presented in a non-academic fashion, with a hot-pink and neon-pink background; I portray myself in an emerald sweatshirt, and my mother is in a deep-blue shirt; the image of me has heterochromia chameleon eyes with a hint of green, while my mother's eyes are blue; both of us have pale skin. I envisioned the picture being exhibited in a pink room with a hand-drawn dotted line that's meant to serve as my vision of the progress of art, from a grey zone in history, to a heterogenous unity, to a breaking point, and to the current dispersion of the spectrum of gay, queer, feminist and other intersectional art.

The painting was stolen from my apartment at the beginning of the full-scale invasion, as were many of the other works I left behind. This sort of act can be perceived as a sort of 'private-room erasure' of personal queer experiences and history, dealing a further blow to the solidarity of the community as a whole – because erasure isn't limited to one person, but affects all the complex concepts, cause-and-effect relationships, realities, consequences and history of the entire group. (Just as the current war cannot be distilled to merely 'Ukraine against Russia', 'A conflict of modernity', 'Putin's war', 'A political question' or 'The south and west of Ukraine'.)

The thief probably didn't have any idea about the meaning behind my painting, but they still chose to take it. This in itself reveals another form of composite erasure of queer people (and other groups) – being wilfully ignorant that something exists at all, or feeling that something about it renders it valueless. (Just as Western narratives about 'Giving up territory', 'Diplomatic negotiations on any terms', 'Saving the face/name of the governing state', 'Making phone calls' demonstrate a devaluing of lived experiences and the strength of the erasure machine that's integral to hypocritical Western humanism, and the blindness, naïveté, futility, fragility and outright harmfulness of the corrupted Western perception of 'peace' and 'the future'.)

Sem'ya could be considered physically lost, but this doesn't mean that it has disappeared or ceased to exist, stopped carrying a queer meaning or opposing the rotten heteronormative perception of the world. (Just as the occupation of territories does not signify their loss, does not mean we have forgotten them, and 'silence' in occupied cities does not indicate peace or compliance. The south, the east, Crimea – they are Ukraine, our home, our queer land. Every day the battle there continues.)

Ultimately, like a planet that's facing the erasure of living organisms, flora and fauna, queerness will prevail, if it is the last thing it does. (Just as Ukraine will win, because it's the only thing that's left for it to do.)

TANYA G

Fireworks Will Never Sound the Same

1

i think they've used up all of their rockets
now we just have to survive
chemical weapons
maybe ten atomic bombs
that's it
my little brother stated with relief and
fell asleep

2

BLACK CAT OF ABNEY PARK

i woke up to a shadow at my bedside
it told me not to be afraid
that soon i will know for certain who i am
and who i must never become

3

i've grown wary of the night
night-time means life or death
alarm every half an hour
checking the blue screen
air raid alert
air raid alert
air raid alert
u ok?

4

i lay awake in my childhood bedroom waiting every night for
    the explosions and warplanes and
they never come but the fear always lingers

since i was fourteen it stayed
i am twenty-two and my home is on fire and i am far away
    and reading the news, false threats, troops at the border
have a smoke and not know where you'll be in a year

5

END?

i can feel my memories of home fading. there have been times i've been away for a year, but this one is different because everything is different. a glimpse of the past stuck on repeat − walking with my sister through the town that raised us, the town in which we no longer live − still the same, even though we're not − talking of change: she said she was afraid every time we come back would be the last. i secretly wish we didn't have this conversation. i think everyone could feel it − feel it breathing down our necks, creeping in with the february wind. the winter is long, cold and dark. the winter can go on for years.

ELLIOTT MISKOVICZ

Tuning the Bandura

Early 1990s, Philadelphia

OCCUPIED LAND OF THE LENNI-LENAPE PEOPLES

red maple, fireflies

SATURDAYS

I feel at home amongst this gathering of Jews who recently left Kazakhstan, Azerbaijan, Ukraine – these various lands are disentangling from Russia, yet its language still echoes in their mouths. I hear some of their children call my father 'Dyadya' (Uncle), and for the first time I learn about chosen family.

PURIM

There's vodka in the punch bowl. Older Ukrainian women surround the piano, belting out songs. Their unhindered confidence leaves a mark on me. Folding poppy seeds into tri-angles of dough, I learn about armed resistance to genocide.

2020, Buxton, Oregon

OCCUPIED LAND OF KALAPUYA, SILETZ

AND ATFALATI PEOPLES

huckleberry, northern spotted owl

Pandemic winter in a forest of moss and ferns.

Shabbat candles lit, phones off, walking the foggy trails.

Havdalah candles lit, phones back on, the new week begins. Voices resonate through shared walls as we overhear each other's video calls: meetings with prison abolitionist groups; another work training session; my weekly hour-long calls with Oryst in Ukraine. His laughter at my mispronunciations of words.

Yahrzeit candles lit by the window, we feed our beloved dead.

TU BISHVAT

An intimate gathering of trans anti-Zionist Jews, huddling under the shelter of cedar branches. On this holiday meant for honouring trees, we lament the uprooting of olive trees in Palestine. Through masked mouths, we say, 'Not in our name.'

Melted snow. End of lease. Packing up our altars again. The Jewish tradition of constant uprooting.

Summer 2022, Poland

Hundreds of bottles of herbal medicines, packed into boxes like bodies on a crowded train. Herbs to help with sleep, with stress, with pain. Hawthorn, skullcap, valerian, rose, lavender... familiar plant friends in this unfamiliar place.

We carry the boxes down flights of stairs, load them on to a van, and later stack them by the table at the evacuation point near the border of Ukraine.

Hours pass as we press the small bottles into the hands of hundreds of evacuees, with prayers that these herbs might lighten the heaviness of their travels.

Dusk arrives. These medicine boxes are a little lighter now. When we get back we carry the boxes back up stairs to be refilled. In Lublin, then in Warsaw. Repeat. Repeat. Repeat.

The Ukrainian tradition of constant uprooting.

Early 2000s, Tucson, Arizona

OCCUPIED LAND OF O'ODHAM AND

HOHOKAM PEOPLES

saguaro cactus, horned lizard

We arrive at the community centre with our rucksacks packed for the week, and catch a ride to the border with a silver-haired immigration activist named Glenn. I'm sat with my high-school best friend in the back seat; we lean forward, listening to her stories. While she drives us through the dusty roads of the Sonoran Desert she tells us the hidden histories of these terrains. Hearing her recount tales of the Apache Wars of the 1800s, I once again learn about armed resistance to genocide.

Dawn rises, the sun already screaming like a baby torn from his mother. We head out on the rocky trails, rucksacks full of medicine in case we meet an injured traveller. In each hand we carry heavy jugs to hide under desert shrubs. Water in the desert.

With markers we write notes on packs of socks for the migrating families we hope will find them. They walk through the night to avoid getting caught and caged. Glenn scribbles '*¡Agua Pura! ¡Bendiciones!*' ('Pure water! Blessings!') on the jugs while we place snack bars on the rocks beside them, offering prayers that this nourishment might lessen the deadliness of their travels.

We stumble on a pile of dried bones lying on the sand. For a moment we aren't sure if they're the bones of an animal or of a human child, like the skeleton this same group of volunteers found earlier in the month. No end to genocide or blood spilled in the desert.

Dusk arrives. The weight of our packs is a little less now. Heading back to camp, we discover that some of the jugs we left out earlier have been slashed with knives and emptied by Border Control agents.

Early 1990s, Philadelphia

My dad switches back and forth between Dr Jekyll and Mr Hyde.

Dr Jekyll Dad lights up on one of our trips to the Ukrainian deli on Bustleton Avenue, when I show him how I can read the tiny candy wrappers now. Despite overhearing Ukrainian as a child, the language never stuck for him. Elated, he squeezes my small hands.

One day, Dr Jekyll Dad brings home a bandura for me – a family heirloom of one of his friends from Ukraine. Beaming, he tells me the importance of this instrument to our ancestors. After a generation of assimilation, I'm a spark of hope for repairing the broken link.

I touch the ornate patterns around the edges, smell the wood. I wrap my arms around its large body like an embrace, pluck its deep strings, feel them reverberate through me. Despite the intimidating number of strings, something about this instrument feels like home.

I don't want to talk about Mr Hyde.

January 2022, Tucson, Arizona

The only Ukrainian deli in town, run by Olga the Matriarch.

My obvious queerness creates no border between us.

'I might not go to Ukraine this summer any more, if this looming invasion happens,' I say.

She looks at me intently. 'It's definitely not going to happen,' she says. 'There's nothing to worry about.'

'I hope so,' I say.

Early 1990s, Philadelphia

I write secret notes using the Cyrillic alphabet to Svitlana and Ulyana after Shabbat service. Their childhoods were spent in Ukraine, but they have been recently uprooted, and we reach for common ground in language.

2020, Oregon

I have different secrets now. I exchange them with Oryst, almost telepathically. He lives in Dnipro, Ukraine, nine hours in the future. My mornings, his evenings.

We first bonded as two fags with shared interests in weird music, revolutionary histories and language, seeming never to run out of things to talk about. We met by happenstance but immediately recognised each other, in that mysterious way that shrivels scepticism around the possibility of past lives. Our physical distance helped override our inhibitions, making it easier to expose our raw, unfiltered confessions over rambling voice memos.

During the pandemic lockdowns, we became each other's confidants, talking every day, sometimes in Russian, sometimes in English, often for hours.

Invisible tendrils stretch across oceans.

February 2022

Oryst doesn't want to speak in Russian any more. I understand.

Early 1990s, Philadelphia

My uncle, once fluent in Russian, tells me about his first trip to Russia. He holds back details from my innocent ears, says they'd cause nightmares – multiple days of interrogation and detainment, that's all I know. A trauma which rinsed the Russian out of his mouth. He never spoke the language again after that.

This uncle, the carrier of our ancestral stories. Passing down his obsession, he invents little games to imprint me with the details of their lives.

2011

That same uncle tells me it was a disgrace that I showed up to my grandmother's funeral 'dressed in drag'. He says he doesn't understand why I stopped talking to my father so long ago. He says a lot of things. We never speak again after that.

2022

I have a big queer chosen family now, and it reaches to Ukraine. Oryst says he feels like we are brothers.

2013, Oregon

There are five of us cackling around the kitchen table, faggot friends between revolutions. Our bodies are so at ease together they collapse into a woven tangle of contact: his arm, overloaded with bracelets, wrapped around their black-lace shoulders; their fishnet-clad legs propped up on his thigh, exposed by short-shorts; his turquoise nails rest on her head of curls, which lies in my lap.

Suddenly our cackling takes a strange turn. Someone makes a joke about gulags. I'm not laughing. I ask questions. These are smart people who I trust, involved in labour-union organising, international solidarity and liberation movements.

They explain that the bad things we hear about the USSR are just US propaganda. That the only people sent to gulags were oppressive capitalists who refused to give up their wealth and control. That those orchestrated genocidal famines were actually just a result of foreign sanctions. That it was only rich people and conservatives who didn't like the USSR.

I'm perplexed. The people I grew up around who fled the USSR were poor and working class. Still, I question what I know. I question what my family told me when I was growing up. *My family is religious, Zionist, right-wing… I don't trust their perspectives on practically anything else… can I trust what they said about the USSR?*

Questioning my reality: this is something I was trained to do. For a moment I'm silent and confused. I soon regret this.

24th February 2022

2:58 A.M. DNIPRO, 5:58 P.M. TUCSON

Oryst: They might invade from the north. God, I am freaking out. I'm in full panic mode.

Me: I wish I could hug you. You can call me if you want to talk. Like you said, I'm much further from it than anyone else you know.

Oryst: OK, I will call you. That will probably help me. <3

Me: Sorry, I got disconnected. The internet isn't reaching my trailer.

Oryst: It's OK. Thanks for talking. <3

Oryst: I'm shaking. Russia has declared a 'military operation' against Ukraine. There are explosions in Dnipro.

Thank you so much for all the support. <3

Right now we are leaving our apartment to go to Ada's grandmother's basement. We will try to get out of the country if it's possible. They've invaded from all sides. There are bombings in western cities. Nowhere seems to be safe. I feel trapped. The hours feel like weeks.

Me: Fuck. I just woke up. I tried to call you...

Oryst (*Sends a series of videos of running to a bomb shelter with Ada*): I love you. And I just wanna say... we're going to win! And you will come to Ukraine this summer. And we will have a great time. Thank you for being my support right now. Good night. <3

February–April 2022,
Tucson, Arizona

Less than 24 hours in, and the profound alienation is already setting in. I can barely eat or sleep. I check for updates around the clock. Everyone around me is confused. No one relates to what I'm going through. There's a gulf of silence when I try to talk about it.

I rapidly lose respect for dozens of activists I formerly admired all across this continent. For the most part, when people in these extensive 'radical' communities talk about Ukraine, it's only one of two things:

1. They parrot Russian propaganda's bullshit excuses for the invasion.
2. They *exclusively* criticise the mainstream media's double standards about covering Ukraine, with no mention of how absent the coverage has been for the past twenty years about Russia's invasions of Georgia, Moldova, Crimea, Donetsk, Luhansk... which emboldened Russia to take it to this point.

In either case, they include zero criticism of Russia, and zero empathy for Ukrainians. Masks fall from faces, revealing those who care more about virtue signalling or edgy aesthetics than leading with a basic compassion for humanity. *What happened to our values of self-determination, anti-colonialism and defence against Fascism?*

I lose confidence in knowing who is safe any more. Questioning who is safe – this is something I was trained to do.

I find ways to channel my panic and rage. I organise fundraisers for my friends to escape Dnipro, or to acquire weapons to defend Kyiv. I work day and night to counter the rampant disinformation and conspiracies plaguing my community around this war, which silence or ignore Ukrainian voices. I record and publish audio interviews, compile resource lists, create infographics.

I engage in countless difficult conversations, including heated arguments with some of my closest friends. Some of the queers who I had considered chosen family now actively spread the lies of this fascist empire that is committing genocide against my people. We don't talk right now: a familiar familial experience.

In the midst of all this alienation, I decide to search for anyone in my local sphere who might want to collaborate. I write to huge networks of Tucson activists, forums of hundreds of people.

Aside from being harassed by pro-Russian communists, the main response comes from two people whose Polish grandparents fled Russian terror. Despite our slim numbers, we get busy. We hang posters, print and distribute zines, promote events, hand out flyers in the street, drop banners over the highway.

April heatwaves send me back to Oregon, where I team up with an old friend there who is first-generation Estonian. They're the only person I know in all of Turtle Island who shares my deep rage towards Russian imperialism in such a personal way, hitting so close to home.

Talking with them is like a drink of water in the desert.

27th February 2022

I still don't know a single other person on this continent who knows anyone living in Ukraine. In my sleepless grief and constant fear I feel entirely alone.

I find myself weighing the trauma of this invasion next to the trauma of my childhood. After debating it for a while, I decide to reach out to my estranged father who I haven't talked to in over a decade. When you're searching for water in the desert it doesn't matter how dirty the water is.

He answers the phone, says he's at the birthday party of a Georgian family, and they just made a toast to Ukraine. Grief swelling up in his community, they still find ways to celebrate. He speaks of loved ones in Odesa and Kyiv who are escaping to Romania – names I remember from my childhood: I see their faces in my mind, standing in lines at the border.

He brings up the lies of the Russian media, saying, 'It reminds me of when I was a teenager and we would listen to Radio Moscow on short wave. Also all lies!'

He talks about how there are no gay rights in Russia, and how bad it will be for trans people if Russia occupies Ukraine. I'm shocked. *My transphobic, anti-gay, estranged father understands this and is concerned about it? But my queer activist communities at home don't? What is this new inverted reality I'm living in? I usually disagree with my dad about practically everything… Now I agree with him, while disagreeing with most of my friends?*

I remember the message I got the day before from David, an artist in Kyiv: 'I will probably join the territorial defences instead of the anarchist detachment tomorrow. It's more convenient for me. Now a lot of feminists, gays, queers, Jews, Muslims, people of all political views are joining the Ukrainian army.'

A uniting force is blooming around defending Ukraine. Like the Apache Wars, like the Jews in the Achaemenid Empire, like in Palestine today, this is the people's armed resistance to genocide.

In the coming weeks, I continue to keep in touch with my estranged father. He sends me videos from a 'Solidarity with Ukraine' interfaith prayer rally in Philly, where he was invited to give a speech.

He reminds me that he still has my bandura in his attic. I see it in my mind: the strings warping out of tune, the bridge gathering dust, the hole of the soundboard yawning like a mouth. He invites me over to collect it, to bring it back to life.

I realise I'm still afraid to enter his house.

15th July 2022, Warsaw, Poland

I don't speak any Polish. I'm supposed to be going to language school in Ukraine. I'm supposed to be with Oryst. I had changed my ticket destination from Kyiv to Warsaw, hoping that by the summer it might be safe enough to take the train to Ukraine from there.

Instead, today, Oryst tells me that a missile just landed very close to his house in Dnipro again. Almost five months of knowing he could get killed by Russians at any moment. I'm getting used to hearing air-raid sirens in the background of his voice messages.

I go to an event at the Ukrainian cultural centre in Warsaw. I have plans to finally meet with this group of queer anti-colonial activists from Ukraine who I've been corresponding with for months.

One of them also has family in Dnipro. When I greet her, she's shaken up by the news of the recent attacks there. Her mother watches missiles fly past her window. We hug and I start sobbing. This is the first time I'm in physical contact with someone who understands the visceral panic of this ongoing nightmare.

The next morning I rush out to meet them at a protest at the Russian embassy, thinking only a dozen of us will be there. I'm wrong – there are thousands, flooding the streets.

Monsoon in the desert.

23rd July 2022,
Lemko Region, Poland

I'm near the village where many of my Lemko relatives are buried. After debating it for a while, I finally reach out to my uncle – the one who carries our family stories. We talk for the first time in over a decade.

On the first night of the Lemko gathering, a folk choir performs a memorial concert dedicated to Ukraine. Finally, I'm able to let out some more of the tears I've been holding back for months.

The next morning, there's a commemoration of Operation Vistula, the forced resettlement of Lemko and Boyko Ukrainians by Soviet authorities. I end up in a conversation with two brothers whose grandparents were deported by this operation. One of them looks at me sharply and says, 'Back then, 150,000 Ukrainians were forced to leave their homes because of Moscow. Now today, seven million Ukrainians are forced to leave their homes – again because of Moscow.'

We stand together in silence for a moment. The silence is interrupted by a woman plucking a bandura on the stage.

The sound of raindrops in the desert.

Listening to the bandura, I think about the Jewish diaspora. No matter where we are in the world, we keep singing our songs. Tyrants across centuries have displaced us from our homes and taken our lives, but they can never take away our songs. To carry these songs forward is an act of resistance. For Ukrainians, this is also the story.

1870s–1930s, Galicia, Ukraine

Friday after sunset. Marúsya digs the bandura out from under the floorboards. Despite the ban on this instrument as part of Russia's attempt to bury Ukrainian culture, Marúsya's family has successfully kept the outlawed heirloom from sight. Although her uncle's eyes were gouged out by Tsarist authorities for plucking these forbidden strings, the instrument's hidden body remains unscathed.

A family of sheep look at Marúsya strangely as she carries the bulky instrument across the pasture to her neighbour's house. She hears their voices sing in Yiddish through the door, and they welcome her in with warmth. After rekindling the fire in their oven, she begins to play.

Decades pass. Marúsya's grandchild, Kvitka, carries the instrument to the back room of the village shul. The Jewish battalion of the Ukrainian Galician Army is gathered there, ritually preparing to defend their homes from Russian invaders who carry red flags. Kvitka nervously improvises a melody in the Altered Dorian scale. Soldiers huddle in a circle around her, feel the vibrations through the floor.

More years pass. Kvitka plays an old lullaby to her newborn on the bandura. Her hands shake, aware that if she is caught playing the instrument she might be away to a forced-labour camp.

The bandura still lives under the floorboards. The music carries on.

Early 1990s, Philadelphia

The sixty-four strings bend and stretch, sliding in pitch with each slight turn of its wooden pegs. This bandura doesn't know it yet, but far in the future I will dig her out of the attic, wipe off the dust and bring her home. For now, my child-sized hands fumble over the many strings, plucking them clumsily with curiosity and hope.

Each string is an individual in a family, all bound to the same home. Some strings resonate in harmony with each other; some create harsh dissonance; some are wound tight, on the verge of snapping and breaking. All of them shift over time.

With gratitude:
To Vlada, who pushed me to write for this book despite my relative safety, and insisted on claiming me as Ukrainian.
To Jai, and all the indigenous teachers in my life who keep showing me that uprooting colonialism comes from the inside out.
To Yevhenii, who opened my eyes and heart to the complex histories of Ukraine.
To the land I live on, and the ancestors of this land.
To my Lemko ancestors, who keep loudly calling me home.

TARAS GEMBIK

Queerstitution

At the Solidarity Community Centre, 'Slonecznik' ('Sunflower') – a space at the Museum of Modern Art in Warsaw, which was converted into a crisis centre where we gave legal advice – we made 2–3,000 sandwiches daily, and delivered them to Warsaw's train stations or bus stops. We also organised poetry readings, trying to find the words to express the unspeakable – the brutality of war, the experiences of exile and uprooting – which seems like an immense trial. How can something so intimate, so wreathed in metaphor, become a form of resistance and an act of discord? Today, poetry demands our collective memory, our rage and solidarity, for in times of war the critical content and communal existence of poetry are inseparable (I will elaborate upon literature later) amongst many other things, which we continue doing to this day.

The very first volunteers who came to help us prepare the sandwiches were LGBTQI+ individuals – friends, acquaintances, members of the community. Maybe – or, the way I see it, most certainly – we currently lack the kind of institution that's dedicated to a Ukrainian LGBTQI+ context, an institution that would study, examine, analyse everything that happened during Ukraine's colonisation by Russia, and how free queers fought, are fighting, will keep fighting, so we must create this institution ourselves.

It is interesting to observe the shift away from the socially enforced stereotypes of 'hypersensitivity', 'curiosity', 'trendiness' towards a distinct position – from the queer army to the countless hours of volunteer work in the masculine traditions which we were so scrupulously raised with (perhaps not everyone, but I definitely was) – inculcated in us not by family, but through the social system.

There's a real deconstruction taking place of narratives where the word 'queer' doesn't signify something vague, but transforms into a call for change. We need new practices and theories, and today we're creating them – we're fighting, each on our own personal fronts; we're unbreakable, and our victory is getting closer and closer!

Lesya Ukrainka Through the Prism of My Volynian Queerness

I first encountered this great – perhaps even the greatest, as great as the Svitiaz Lake (the deepest lake in Ukraine, in Volyn, where both she and I are from) – *Ukrainka* (Ukrainian woman), Lesya Ukrainka, in my youth, and it was one of the encounters that challenged the system which I inhabited. It all began with the heroine of *The Forest Song*,[1] Mavka. She is the embodiment of the bright and humane beginning in a person's life, high poetic dreams and pure love, sincere friendship and the love of freedom. For her, freedom is a natural state, like life, like breathing... like romance. I was approximately fourteen when I first came across her, and her character was cemented inside my subconscious for years to come.

> How can it be that freedom has disappeared?
> Will the wind disappear this way some day?[2]

Afterwards, she delves deeper and deeper into words, where the passion for Polish nature mixed with my clear understanding of who I truly am, impacting my position towards the 'infirm' or 'sick', as she taught me to fight not through the illness that we all know of from school books, but through the total lack of fear in the face of anything.

> Who told you that I am weak,
> That I submit to fate?
> Does my hand shake?
> Are my song and thought frail?[3]

---

1 Lesya Ukrainka, *Lisova Pisnya* (*The Forest Song*) (1912).
https://www.l-ukrainka.name/uk/Dramas/LisovaPisnja.html
2 ibid.

3 Lesya Ukrainka, 'Khto vam skazav, shcho ya slabka...' ('Who Told You that I Am Weak...') (Lviv: Z podorozhn'oyi knyzhky, 1911).

As I became much older, her works helped me build my political awareness. In her early poem, 'Songstress',[1] Ukrainka assures her readers that no forces will make her abandon her duty – to serve her motherland and native people. The young poetess understood that the poetic path is gruelling, and to embark upon it alone is difficult – such ruminations and feelings also imbue her poem 'My Path'.

> Alone, it won't take long for me to lose my way,
> But it is hard to lose it in a team.[2]

She dreamed of using her words to galvanise people into fighting for liberation, for truth, and she knew that this battle could be fatal for many of the fighters – herself included:

> Let me die, but let the sun shine
> Above the people, in its truth and hope![3]

She had the right to say about her poetry: 'My star! The light of your eyelids will be clear',[4] for a person who has chosen such a sharp blade to fight a hated enemy, with words as her weapon, could not help but kindle the fire of love in the hearts of future generations – a love for freedom and a loathing for tyranny.

---

1 Lesya Ukrainka, 'Spivets' ('Songstress') (Lviv: Na krylakh pisen', 1893).

2 Lesya, Ukrainka, 'Mij šl'yah' ('My Path') (Lviv: Na krylakh pisen', 1893).

3 Lesya Ukrainka, 'Son' ('Dream') (Lviv: Na krylakh pisen', 1893).

4 Lesya Ukrainka, 'Zorya poeziji' ('The Star of Poetry') (Lviv: Dumy i mriyi, 1899).

I think it's fitting to end with the words of torment and suffering she set on paper:

> I would like to go out into the open field,
> Fall face down on the wet soil,
> And cry so loud that the stars would hear me,
> That people would be horrified by my tears.[1]

---

1 Lesya Ukrainka, 'Horyt' moje serce, joho zapalyla…' ('My Heart Burns, it Was Lit…') (Lviv: Dumy i mriyi, 1899).

DIMETTRA

How I Spent My Summer

Part I: 'My Perfect Summer Day'

The hot summer sun of Paris burns my legs, waking me at one p.m. I jump up with a start, dreading the thought of oversleeping and missing my flight to Berlin. I only have one hour to pack and get to the airport. As per usual, I'm running late. Sasha hates it when I'm late, and the night before she specifically reminded me to set an alarm... but my aunt didn't wake me up – both of us have overslept.

We land in Berlin and are greeted by Boji, who is voguing, and Sasha, who is running, balanced on heels and has an insane hairstyle, screaming, 'GIIIIRLIIIES!'

We go to some local art sale, drink Club-Mate, meet some cool people.

After that, we party all night long.

The sound of air-raid sirens wakes me up. I don't hide any more – I've got used to them. But I wake up to rain in Lviv, and understand that Paris and Berlin was all a dream.

I have breakfast – a cigarette and a coffee. I get dressed – fabulously, painting my face a bit – and walk out into the street, into the psychological (but no longer only psychological) battlefield. Dressing up and doing my make-up is the only thing I have left – I can no longer self-actualise the way I did before. Sometimes I don't even want to.

At the beginning of the full-scale invasion I began to rearrange my wardrobe, jewellery, cosmetics, nail polish, etc., as I left my things behind at my previous apartment when I moved from Kyiv to Lviv – all my costumes and usual outfits, all my decorations, all my adornments, my make-up. A month after the war started, after the tensions in the country had slightly eased up, I decided to collect my belongings. I messaged my previous landlord, but he said that they threw everything away – *everything*!

I cried, I screamed, I couldn't breathe. It still haunts me now – it was a hugely significant part of my life.

I head off to my favourite café to drink some tea and relax, dressed in a way that brings me comfort.

On the way I head past a playground, where a bunch of kids are hanging around – they're probably about 15–18 years old. My friends and I call this playground 'the walk of shame'. As I pass, I hear them screaming at me: 'Pirate, where's your ship?' (Maybe because I'm wearing a *hustynka*, which from afar probably looks a little like the bandanas pirates wear?) Sometimes I get the impression they know more swear words and derogatory terms than I do.

'Faggot! Ew, why do you do this shit? What, you've got nothing better to do? Oh, you have a dog? Are you going home to fuck it?'

Often people who pass me are having conversations amongst themselves, but they immediately stop talking when I enter their field of vision, and look at me as if I'm covered in shit, or as if I have a big sign on my head that says 'stare at me in an extremely condemnatory manner'. People with kids grab them by their hands and lead them further away from me. Maybe I'm a leper – maybe they're afraid I'm sick and I'll somehow infect their children… Of course homosexuality is an airborne disease…

The children in the playground come over and surround me, laughing at me loudly and pointing their fingers like we're at the zoo. This is nothing new – I'm used to having people pay attention to me, and in most cases it manifests itself in the most illogical, aggressive, intolerant modes of behaviour.

I don't dignify these exclamations with a response, and just keep pretending that they don't exist. But they do exist – they inflict deep injuries. I feel like I'm almost fighting for the right to be a part of this world, fighting for the right to peacefully take up space on the street and to wear whatever I please without having to think, 'Will I get killed for this? Is this too provocative?'

I try to abstract myself from reality, but these people leave indelible marks on my psyche.

I begin to feel ashamed of walking past servicemen and the police after my friends and I were harassed by the territorial defences. They should have been protecting their territory from dangerous individuals, from occupiers, from the real enemies of Ukraine. But according to them, I'm the real enemy of Ukraine – I'm a faggot. When the war ends, they assured us, when they've killed all the Russians, they'll exterminate us – the faggots – because we're a curse, a disgrace.

Later I'm stopped by the police, who are supposed to be patrolling the area and ensuring some kind of order, who think they're entitled to scroll through my photo gallery, openly ridiculing me for the selfies they find.

Does a uniform mean they have the right to do absolutely anything?

I try to ask them what they're looking for, but I'm only greeted with, 'Shut your mouth, faggot, or I'll write you a notice and take you down to the station. They'll tell you everything there, all right!'

One day, when I walked past some servicemen – I was wearing a bright-green mesh long-sleeve top and my make-up was visible – they started speaking loudly amongst themselves, saying, 'Ew, fuck, look! Should we give her a summons?'

Another day, another group of soldiers cut in front of me and yelled, 'And we're out there dying for you freaks?'

I see these same phrases circulating online, on social media, in the comments on posts by my friends, where right-wing radicals try to scare us, threaten to murder us, tell us they'll find us and kill us after the war.

I want to walk calmly, to look how I like, not thinking about being beaten or killed. I'm beautiful and intelligent. I'm talented and sensible. I want to self-actualise and live in peace, in comfort, not thinking, 'Is it OK to look this way? Is it too much?' I'm not a danger to society. I'm not a danger to you or your children. I'm not sick or infectious. I'm a member of this community. I'm brave. I'm Ukrainian!

But the vast majority of my nation sees me as a threat, a freak, a sick person who doesn't have the right to be Ukrainian, who doesn't have the right to live on this earth.

Now, life is simply part of the background. Sometimes it seems like time is stretched out; other times it seems to shoot past in one day – one really horrible day.

I believe the day will come when I will live in a free Ukraine. Free from everything that prohibits people from developing. Free from archaic and irrational prejudices. It will be a country where most people will preoccupy themselves with their own lives, and will try to change them for the better, instead of prying into others' lives and saying, 'That's not right.' Ukrainians love freedom, and I believe that some day this freedom will encompass all spheres of our lives. I believe that there'll be freedom of speech, of thought, of self-expression, of human rights – and that these rights will be protected by those whose duty it is to uphold them, and not infringed.

I believe.

T

Entry (3rd May 2022)

Who are we if not torch bearers? Who are we if not embalmers, morticians, undertakers? We bury our loved ones in backyards and parking lots; pull them out of mass graves and dress them anew. We hold them for too long before they depart, still suspended inside the thick treacle of disbelief, still shuddering from the aftershocks of loss. It's all we're used to; it's all we know.

We anticipate another announcement of an atrocity the likes of which have never been seen before. Elsewhere, the next generation of queer children play hopscotch under a cloudless sky. Their parents watch over them without fear. Their relatives are at work, not stationed at the frontline. Their loved ones are a phone call away, not hiding in occupied homes, occupied streets, occupied cities. Their dogs are running around – tongues out, tails wagging wildly – not cowering from gunshots like fireworks.

They live, and we survive. They laugh, and we bury. Their existence is one of simple joys. But we exist in a mausoleum.

How to Be a War Refugee
in Ten Easy Steps

Step one: Get out alive. Once you've got out alive, convince yourself that you are a traitor to your homeland.

Step two: *Somewhere in Ivano-Frankivsk, a boy turns eighteen. In the morning, he hears his mother's muffled cries through the wall.*

Step three: Learn about survivor's guilt from a healthline.com article. Then read Ilya Kaminsky's work until you're a shuddering, sobbing wreck.

Step four: Send your rich friends (yes, *those* rich friends − the satin-skinned, silver-spoon-fed socialites, whose Bora Bora holidays and Paris fashion-week outfits make you want to tie a noose around your neck) donation links. Block them if they leave you on read.

Step five: Repeat step four over and over, again and again. Congrats! Now you're friendless.

Step six: *Somewhere in Mariupol, a girl teaches her baby brother a magic trick – heat up snow over a fire and watch it transform into water. Now drink, my sweet angel, drink.*

Step seven: Learn to feed yourself anew. Start with canned soup and saltine crackers. When a street vendor offers you half a kilogram of beetroot, don't think about how much you miss your babusya's borscht.

Step eight: Scream at a protest. Keep screaming as the journalist takes your picture.

Step nine: *Somewhere in Odesa, civilians pile sandbags around a monument. You may pummel us with shells and gunfire, but you'll never erase the proof of our existence.*

Step ten: Find someone you love. Hold them tight enough to feel your ribs crack.

Pedigree

You say I mostly speak about imagined horrors, so I sit down and write
a child's obituary.
It's true – I'll celebrate the bruises on my cousin's shoulders
and how they give him reason to believe in fortune;
the wheel that spins, the spectral strings that move us,
the odds that separate the victors
from the corpses.
I wish I could claim ownership of survival,
but last week my dream mother found
a suicide note beneath her pillow.
My living mother found a bullet.

And you can't claim we should've seen this coming
when none of us have asked to be a witness.
When caution is a song we've long stopped humming,
when vigilance is a blood-transmitted sickness.

Entry (25th April 2022)

I wake up and write another war poem. I wield the words like weapons in my hands. The syllables become shrapnel under my skin. Pieces of my flesh have splintered off; got lost in mourning, its ink-black ether. Its deep, murky waters. Its irrevocable pull.

Once again, my appetite is nowhere to be seen. An apple for lunch is a little feast. Once again, I refuse to stay clean. I shower once a week.

Does our agony enthral you? Is our atrophy appealing? Do you want us printed and hung up on every wall, projected on to every screen, exhibited for an audience of leering voyeurs, hungry eyes – the more, the merrier? Will they nod along and offer paltry pleasantries, exchange blank stares? Will they care?

There's no artistry in a massacre, I want to say. It isn't something we write about; it's something we carry. We taste it on the roof of our mouths each time we swallow. We hear an ambulance and think of alarms. We walk along train tracks and think of deportations. And spectating is an act of cruelty.

Instead, I smile and take a bow, get off the microphone, exit the stage. Thank you for coming to this reading. Thank you for listening to the silence between air-raid sirens. Thank you for watching us bleed.

Thank you for watching. Thank you for watching. Thank you for watching.

PROUDLY SUPPORTING
QUEER UKRAINIAN CHARITIES

Proceeds from the sales of this book go to a selection of charities supporting LGBTQI+ people in Ukraine. The list of recipients is periodically reviewed, so that funds go to where they're most sorely needed, but at the time of writing includes:

TU PLATFORM MARIUPOL
(Supporting queer youth)

QUEERS FOR UKRAINE
(Supporting people with HIV in Ukraine and delivering much-needed hormones for the trans community)

INSIGHT NGO
(Humanitarian aid for the LGBTQI+ community in Ukraine)

For more information, links and the most up-to-date list of charities sales of this book support, please visit:

RENARDPRESS.COM/BOOKS/QUEER-UKRAINE